Learning to Write

Kindergarten Tracing Exercises

BABY PROFESSOR
EDUCATION KIDS

Speedy Publishing LLC
40 E. Main St. #1156
Newark, DE 19711
www.speedypublishing.com

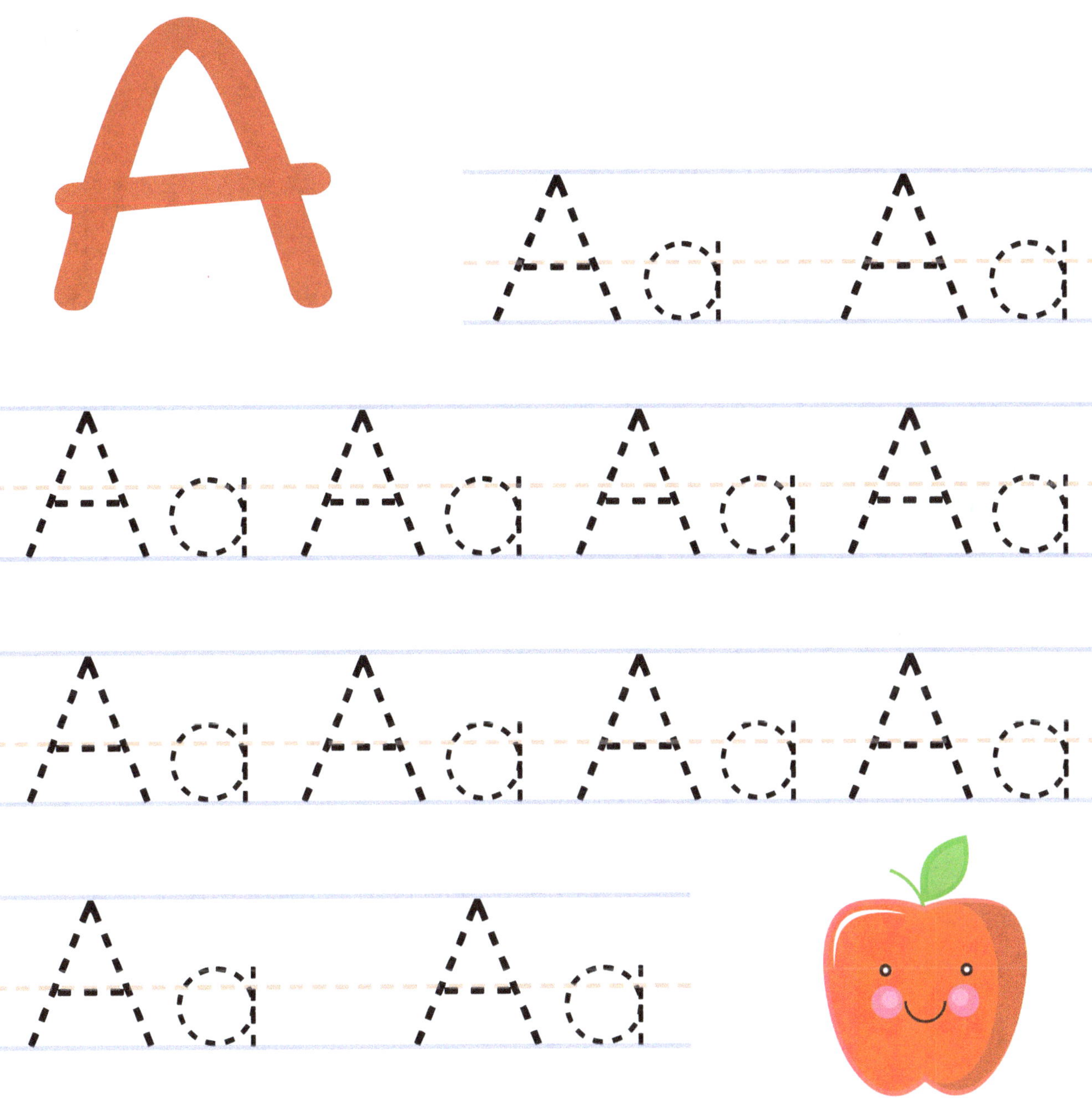

B

Bb   Bb

Bb   Bb   Bb   Bb

Bb   Bb   Bb   Bb

Bb   Bb

C

C c   C c   C c   C c

C c   C c   C c   C c

C c   C c   C c   C c

C c   C c

D

Dd — Dd

Dd Dd Dd Dd

Dd Dd Dd Dd

Dd — Dd

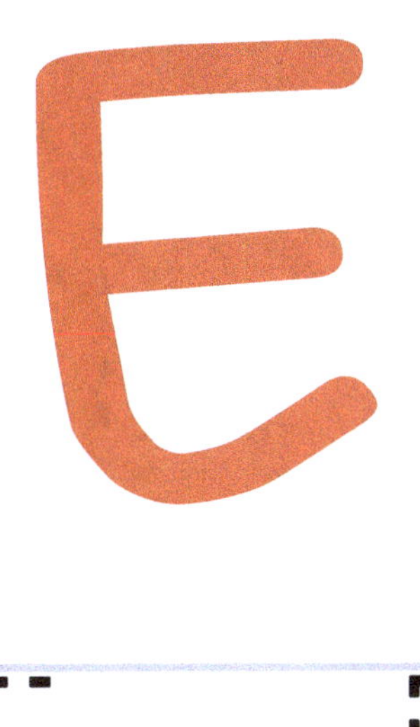

G

H

J

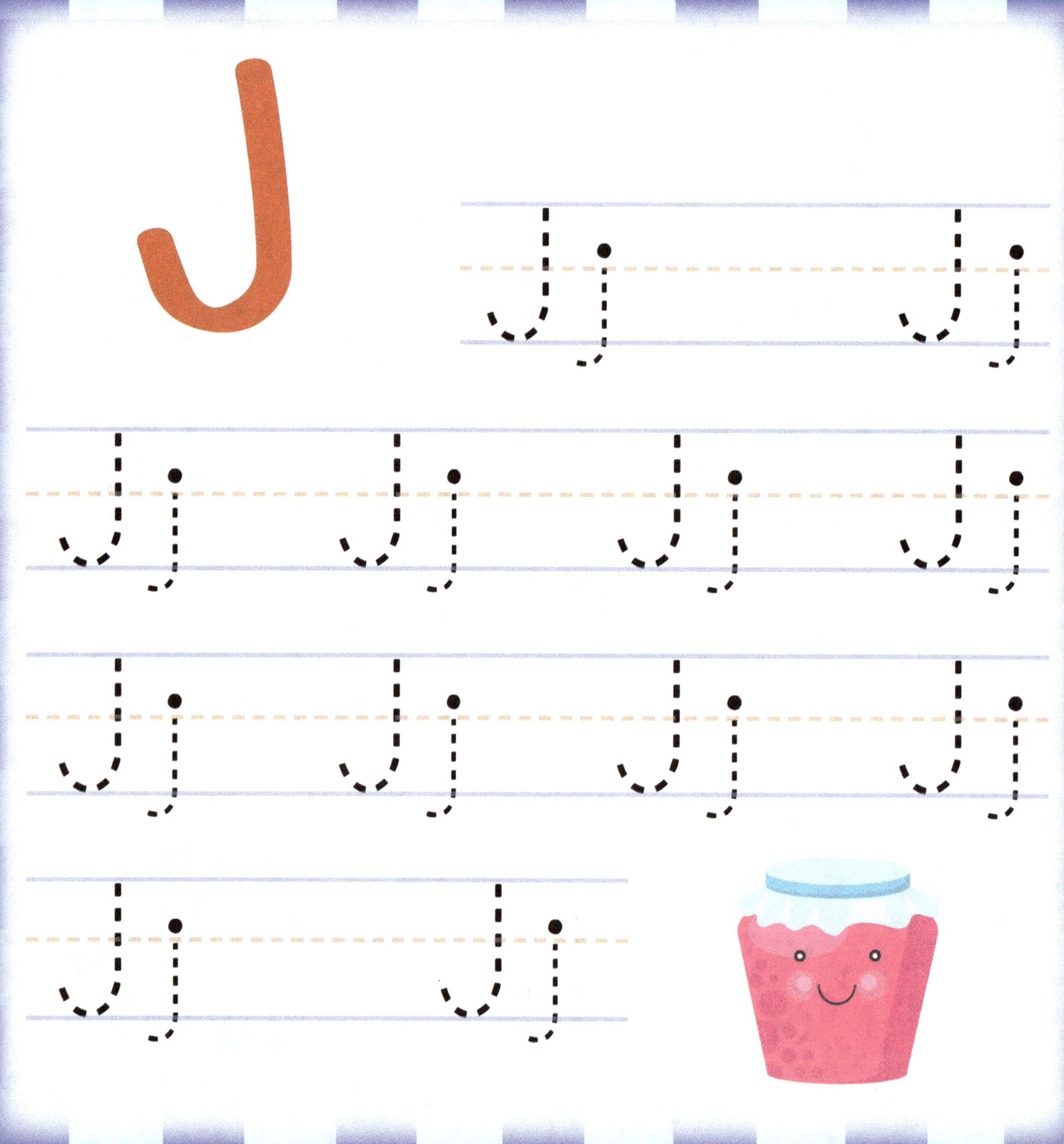

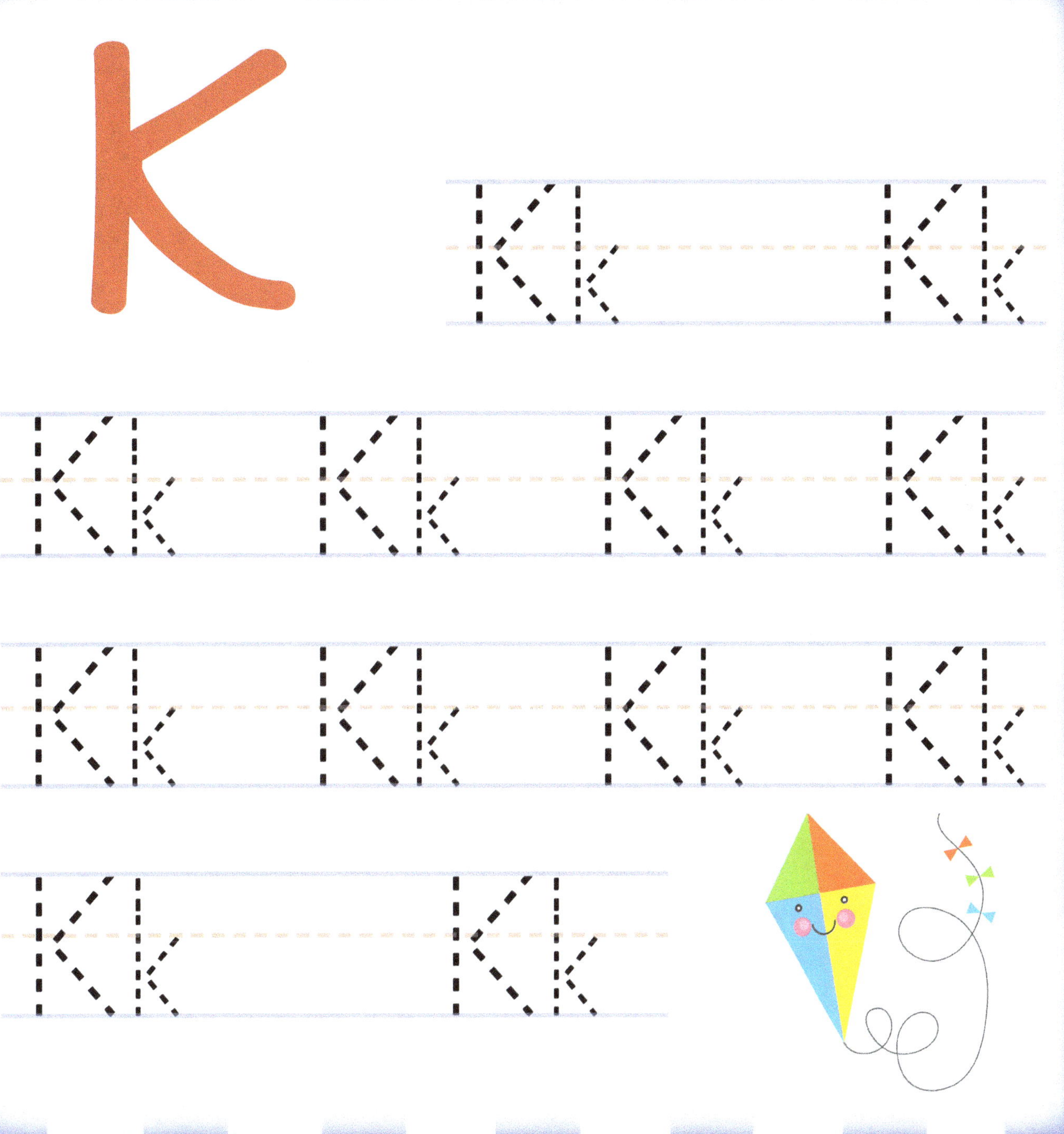
K

  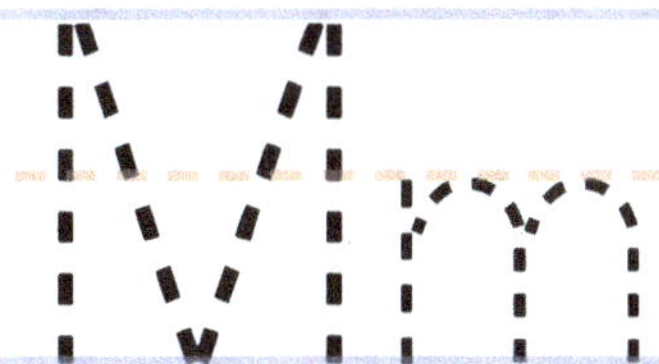

 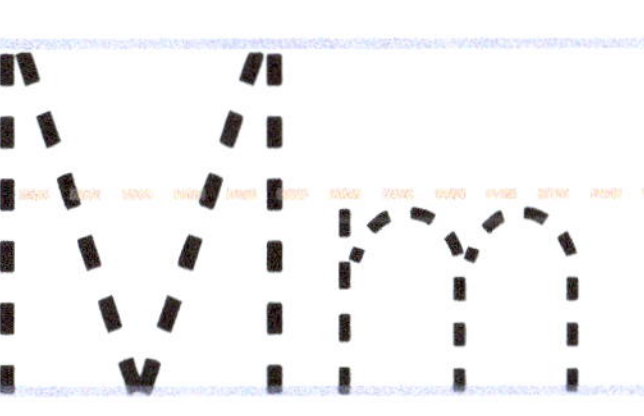 

O

P

Pp Pp

Pp Pp Pp Pp

Pp Pp Pp Pp

Pp Pp

Q

R

Rr   Rr

Rr Rr Rr Rr

Rr Rr Rr Rr

Rr   Rr

S

 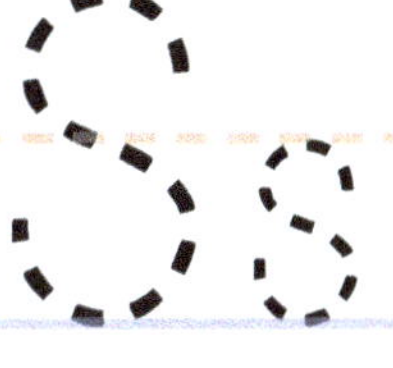  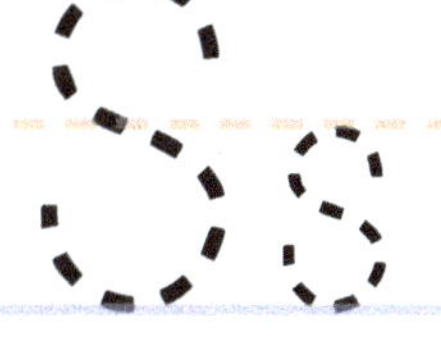

  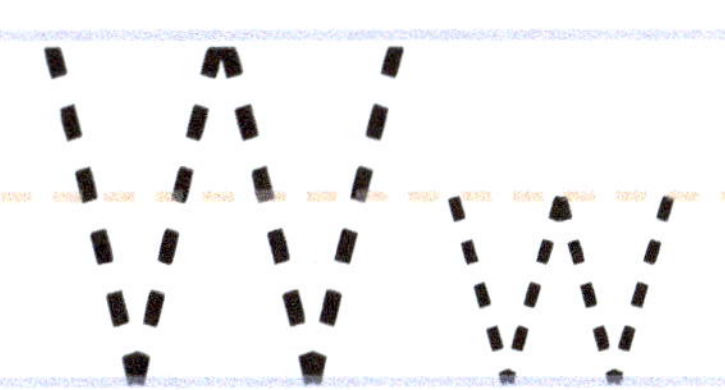

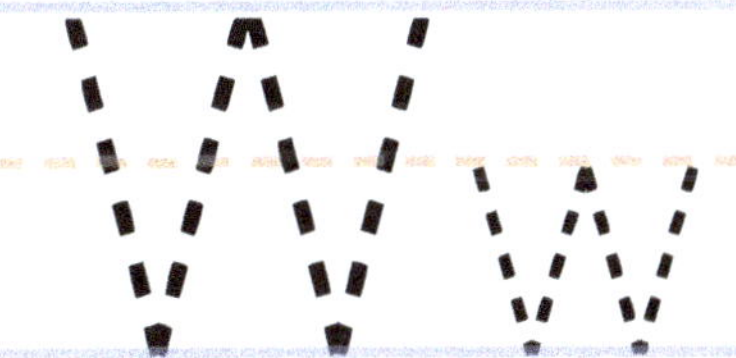  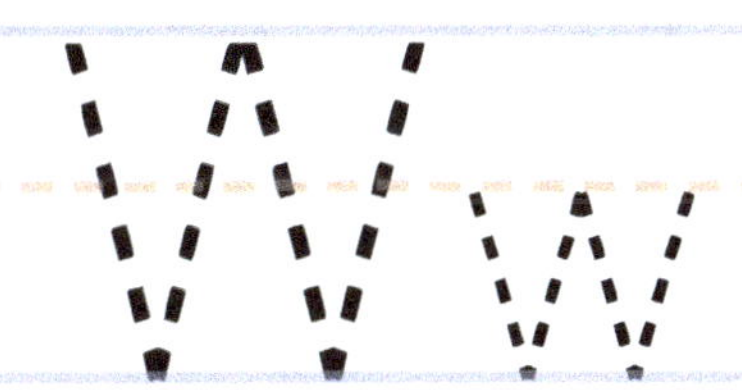

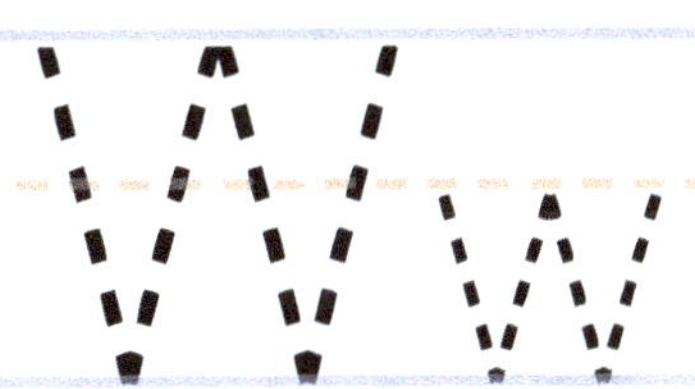 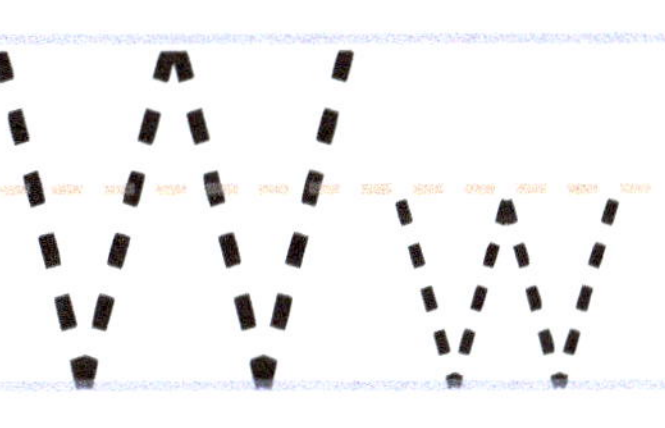 

Z

Write your name on
the blank lines.

The Alphabet

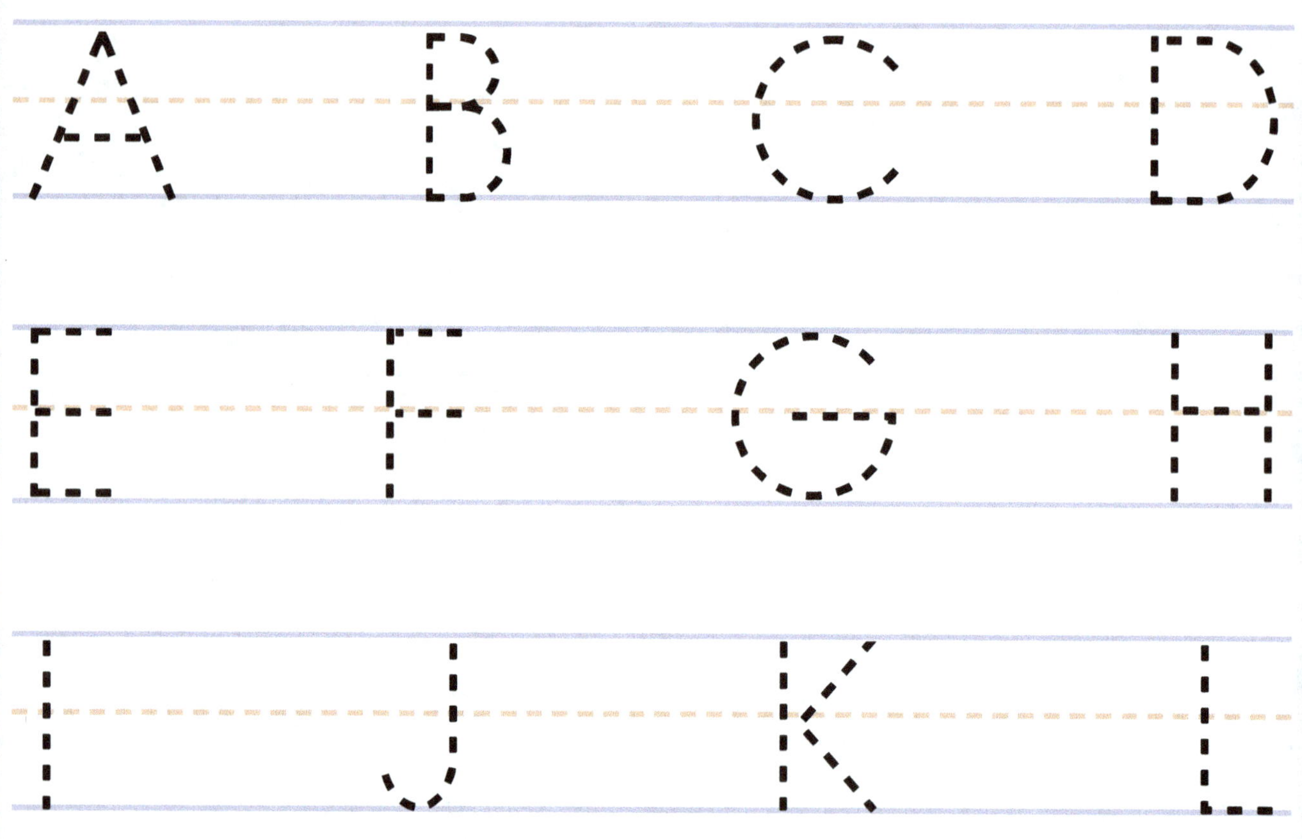

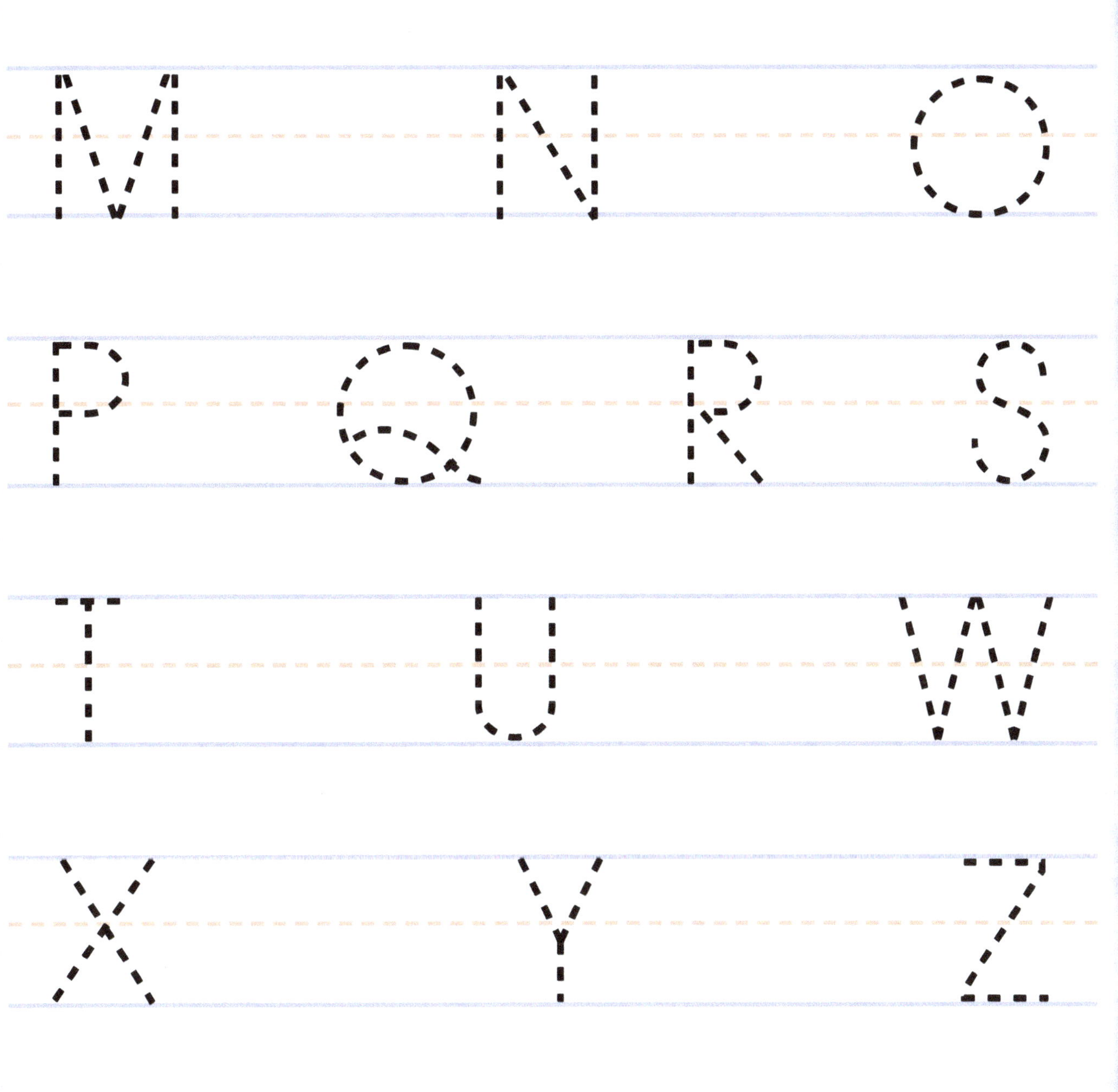

M N O
P Q R S
T U W
X Y Z